EXPRESSIONS OF THE MOMENT

Sean Maile

Expressions of the Moment — Sean Maile

First Edition, January 2019

© 2019 Sean Maile
All rights reserved

Sean Maile
[Poetry] [Poems] [Spirituality]
Expressions of the Moment
Sean Maile, Pages cm—
[First edition]

ISBN / 9781795054843

Book Design — Richard Wehrenberg
richardwehrenberg.com

DEAR READER,

This book of poems was written as expressions of experiences and ideas I have had in different moments of my life. Many of my poems are centered around spirituality and are meant to reflect the introspective awareness experienced through spontaneous moments of meditative contemplations. Many times the profound power of nature and of existence itself has spoken to me through this beautiful world we live in and inspired me to express my understanding through poetry.

I would like you to think of each poem on each page as its own manifestation coming to life in the present moment. It is true that many of my poems share common themes and ideas, but each of them were created in their own unique moment. Poems are not just words written on paper or spoken to a crowd—they are passionate and meaningful expressions that not only reveal much about the poet who creates them; they also reveal deeper aspects of our nature as human beings and of what it means to be alive.

With this book I offer you a glimpse into my psyche and a glimpse of the inspired moments I hold close to my heart as they continuously echo throughout my being. I hope you enjoy these poems and find words that resonate and connect with your own thoughts and experiences. I truly hope that your journey in life is full of growth, understanding, and fulfillment. You have my gratitude and thanks for connecting with me through our shared world we live in.

Sincerely,
SEAN MAILE

EXPRESSIONS
OF THE
MOMENT

Do you understand the potential that hides deep in your being?

Do you think eyes controlled by judgment are truly capable of seeing?

What if you realized that to grow you must truly let go of all you believe and all you think that you know?

Could you free your mind and discover something new?

Could you climb to new heights and expand your point of view?

We have been the cool breeze on hot summer days and the wind that bites during a winter's night in the coldest of ways,

We have raged as waves that rise high in the ocean and existed as gentle streams that a leaf could float in,

We have lived as the fire that burns those who wander too close as they dare and we have been the fire that warms the heart with love and with care,

We have shaken and quaked as the Earth where ground breaks and have also been the Earth that holds up Mankind's weight,

We have transcended time and space as we've traveled to a far-away place,

We have tasted the bitter and sweet and enjoyed both the tastes,

We are all that is, all that was, and all that ever could be,

We are human consciousness expanded so we are all that we should be

Opportunity hides right in front of the eyes,

To live is a chance to grow and to thrive,

Every struggle we face is a chance to strive,

To see the tribulations as teachings is the way of the wise

Look to the skies you find within your mind and shine
with a light that heals mankind,

Deep in your heart is the will to start and you will make
triumph a work of your art,

In the depth of your being is the seed that can grow and
give joy to those who behold the light of your soul,

Deep within is where great potential lies if one looks
with an honest heart then potential comes alive

In the dreaming mind rests a veil of perception where stories and symbols are expressed to invoke personal lessons,

The subconscious mind seeks to teach through the dreams it speaks to the conscious mind while the body sleeps,

In the realm of possibility known through dreams the psyche tries to show a way and a means to balance the internal opposite extremes and promote a growing consciousness bursting at the seams,

Those who sleep with open eyes are the lucid dreamers awake and wise to the fact they are dreaming and they can apply conscious awareness to better understand the dreams meaning and the truths it hides

Through introspective observation a process of realization slowly takes form,

Admiration takes the place of frustration as a fresh perspective reveals the beauty of the raging storm,

Thoughts can pass by much like clouds in the sky if you simply let go, it's easy if you try,

No need to fear the storm's thunder as new revelations offer a different view full of wonder,

Admire the activities of the mind as you allow thoughts you find to drift by at their height as you let the storm pass out of sight,

Thoughts are clouds and you can let them pass by, just let them pass by,

If you like a thought than you can pluck it from the sky, of your minds' eye or just let it pass by, just let it pass by

Gentle beams illuminate the forest canopy as a great truth is expressed and revealed through the gaze of moonlight,

A oneness resides within the evening quiet of the forest that transcends illusions of separation,

Consciousness expands as observation of the power of natures unity reveals the depth of existence,

The joy of being is reflected in the splendor of nature and its enduring beauty that knows no end

Close your eyes and take a deep breath,

Within is the only real frontier mankind has left,

To allow your mind to be taken by the illusions of outer
form is a most dangerous theft,

Deep within lies a power of immeasurable depth,

WE can always change our path if we choose to redirect

The winds of change have been known to re-arrange,

One must learn to accept that nothing stays the same,

Acceptance leads to freedom and the breaking of mental chains,

It's not about how you think life should be, it's about how you play the game

Emotions seem like they flow to and fro,

Fast or slow much like water goes,

They can nurture expression with a current so bold,

They can destroy or create due to the power they hold

Life can be difficult yet we must persevere even when it's hard to cope,

We all must face the dark in our own story though some stories are not spoke,

Do not give in to the dark even if it squeezes until you choke,

We must shine the light that overcomes the dark, shine the light of love and hope

A calm breeze flows through the gentle air of the starlit sky,

At the same moment a soft ray of moonlight reflects the power of natures' mystery,

The serene tones of light gesture solitude in every bit of their illuminated glory,

Those who bear witness are captivated in rapture as the awe-inspiring view expels a peaceful grace

A deep calm overcomes ones senses as inward focus directs an expansion through introspective breath,

We are free to traverse the realm of the infinite as a unity prevails over a separation caused by the veil known as ego,

Consciousness extends beyond limitations as awareness is enhanced through a deepening of collective understanding,

Breathe in the cosmos and breathe out a love that joyfully connects you to all beings in a beautiful state of bliss that knows no end as freedom knows no boundaries

So many live with minds trapped in the past,

The past only exists through memory and was never made to last,

The moment of now is where ones' potential is vast,

So let go of what once was because it has already passed

The moment can be painful and fill your heart with dread,

The moment can also be beautiful and fill you with joy instead,

The freedom of self-realization allows one's shackles to be shed,

But love is the soul food that keeps the spirit fed

A wise old song bird greets the waking world with honesty through fragrant sounds of truth,

In the early morning mist rests a simple beauty as its shroud extends as far as the eye can see,

The dawn bathes all it touches with rays of light and awakens those who slumbered so solemnly through the passing night,

A fresh perspective gives rise to the potential of fresh opportunity as hopes and dreams are birthed by the new days beckoning moments

A sacred journey inward begins as the flow of meditative breath fills ones' center of awareness,

Thoughts fade as a stillness forms within that exists as a profound totality,

A deep reservoir of peace internalizes a return to a balanced state of being,

The power of the wisdom found reverberates outward as it echoes throughout eternity and shines the light of truth

A gust of wind shifts in direction as the gentle dew rests on emerald fields of grass stretching as far and as wide as sight permits the eyes to see,

The morning manifests, as a trance like state of refreshment overcomes the night's soft enchantment,

This moment presents an array of beauty as sights and sounds express a multitude of creative gestures that nature lovingly gifts to all who perceive it,

A forgotten gratitude worthy of humbling the highest mountain peaks is remembered in every day's dawn as nature's power is revealed in its absolute splendor and glory

A shadow of doubt is cast away as the totality of truth takes root and develops a deeper awareness,

Illusions on the surface no longer hold sway as self-realization sharpens the mind's eye and pierces through the veiled projections that lack depth,

Understanding grows as seeds of wisdom planted within ones consciousness begin to bear fruit,

An inner peace resonates and calms the chaos as uncertainty fades and a profound joy is experienced throughout one's being

The heart opens like a flowering bloom as compassion
for all beings takes root and extends from one's center,

Collective awareness gives sight beyond differences
that separate as love permeates the space between self
and others,

An inclusive vision develops as a unified consciousness
grows from infancy toward maturity,

A new stage in human history dawns as the possibilities
of a unified existence expand the freedom of being into
realms beyond imagining

As a mountain sits unmoved, so sits the being of one
who has awakened,

As the wind moves free in all directions, so moves the
being of one who is free from separation,

As water flows effortlessly, so flows the being of one
who understands acceptance,

As fire burns bright in the darkness, so burns the spirit
of one who has found the light within

The eyes give sight to all the glories beheld through ones magnificent vision of life and all its possibilities,

The tongue gives taste to all the unique flavors life offers which wait to be savored,

The ears give understanding to a multitude of sounds forming a symphony that pulsates with experience,

The nose interprets smells that blend together and become the sweet smell of existence,

The flesh allows one to touch and be touched by the joyous mystery of being alive

Love is the sweetest nectar that the human spirit can taste,

Wisdom can guide one through troubled waters and make hardships less difficult to face,

Patience teaches not to rush and that personal growth isn't a race,

No matter the path one chooses to walk in life, one should walk at a natural pace

Through silent meditation the mind can become quiet
much like how a rippling pond naturally stills itself,

Ego vanishes as every meditative breath becomes part
of a transcendence that leads to freedom,

The ego fights with all its power, but is inevitably
guided into a state of slumber as a greater depth is
revealed that goes beyond the ego's superficiality,

This journey proves to be one of peace as inner conflict
is resolved and a lasting joy develops within one's heart

A whisper in the wind slowly culminates into a gesturing echo as the beautiful tones woo the hearts of those who hear it,

The shade offered by the trees combines with the wind's soft wisp to gift a comforting cool respite from the heat of the sun's fiery gaze,

The forest expresses an ancient power of presence as it commands the attention and respect of any who wander into its beautiful terrain,

A return to one's origins is inevitable as natures wisdom inspires a rebirth of the primal self to witness the sacred sanctuary and all its wonders

A state of clarity forms as being in a dream becomes evident and one awakens within the dream while sleeping,

A rush of power surges within one's consciousness due to the understanding that being awake while dreaming creates infinite opportunities to experience unknown depths of existence,

A chance to grasp deeper understanding has arisen as one glimpses truths harder to perceive outside of the dream realm,

Reality bends to the will of the lucid dreamer as they actualize the combining of infinite possibilities found in the dream realm with the conscious awareness experienced in daily waking life

Breathe in and become the state of peace that transcends all things,

Let go of temporary worries and the frustrations worrying brings,

Let your depth express itself as your spirit profoundly sings,

Free yourself from the chains of attachment that are the cause of your sufferings

A variety of elaborate colors fuse into the horizon and mandate attentions to be paid as the sun serenely sets out of sight,

The moons ascension is evident as the night comes into being and the eve begins its promised prosperity,

Stars shine bright as they blanket the lit sky adding a degree of personality to the night's domain,

A time of reflection and quiet observation takes hold as the moments of the night present a stillness that provides a calming sense of clarity

It often seems there is no difference between the mind
that is awake and the mind that dreams,

Consciousness shines bright in either state which can
not go unseen,

Who knows the full reaches of the psyche and what it
all truly means,

The collective energies are like two branches of one
river with different depths in each stream

Through choice many experiences are unknowingly earned,

In every moment exists a deeper lesson to be taught and to be learned,

Some lessons require a bit of pain so don't fret about being burned,

Letting go of how you think life should be can help you find the freedom for which many have yearned

A benevolent awakening ushers in the tide of early morning light,

A rebirth of consciousness occurs as one wakes from a deep state of sleep,

Opportunity mixes with the rising sun to provide awareness of the new day's full potential,

The time to taste the sweetly ripened fruit of existence is always right now in the present moment

Clear your mind if thoughts move ahead or linger
behind,

Be here currently and observe the depth of presence
you find,

To dwell on the past or future can keep you trapped
and confined,

Live focused in the present moment since it is the only
real time

The raging fire burns with a primal desire to engulf all
that it touches,

The flames dance and sway with a captivating
demeanor,

Those watching sit silently as if the fire has taken
command of their senses as they are hypnotized by its
essence,

The elemental power within the fire's center is on
display as its passionate presence blazes through the
darkness of a calm summer's night

Sometimes the best way to find yourself is to find everyone else,

Sometimes the best way to adapt begins with accepting the situation you've been dealt,

Sometimes the best way to understand how you feel is to feel how others have truly felt,

Opportunity for growth is everywhere in life because life is opportunity itself

We have seen galaxies thrive as entire planets come
alive,

We have explored all manner of depths contrived and
gone deep as we dive,

We have observed endings and beginnings as they take
material form,

We have faced all kinds of dangers without ever being
warned,

We have grown and expanded beyond any measure of
rate,

We have chosen to travel beyond any measure of fate,

As eons have passed we have arrived here at last,

Realize there is no need for doubt because you can
achieve any task

The way that some judge others is a reflection upon themselves,

So blinded by subjective judgment that they lost their way and they fell,

So confused by what they project that the truth they can not tell,

Judgment can sweep people up in a river of madness, as it makes the river swell

Take a shooting star as it passes by in the night's sky, place it in your heart and let your heart fly,

Take a soft ray of glowing moonlight, use it as a ray of hope in the dark and let that hope glow bright,

Take a piece of the peace found in the evening's glance, enjoy it as you refuse to leave this moment to chance,

Take solace in the wisdom that sundown brings, it can lift you above the day's worries as if it were your own set of wings

Can you hold the entire world in the palms of your hands with love?

Can you rain compassion on the Earth like clouds rain from high above?

Can you be a living symbol of peace much like a morning dove?

Can you warm others' hearts that have known the cold and give hope to those in need thereof?

Make light your burden as you shed emotional toils you
carry,

Feel an ease overcome your senses as you let go of fears
that keep opportunities buried,

Rise up to new heights as you transcend the pressures
and troubles that vary,

Our greatest journeys are well worth the risk though
they may seem perilous or scary

The sun rises up into the sky as light bathes the morning causing an awakening,

So many different paths to choose to walk as an infinite amount of possibilities present themselves,

Excitement fills the air as every step forward leads to new ground waiting to be explored,

A feeling of wonder overwhelms the senses as the grandiosity of existence echoes throughout the present moment

The sands of time can be set adrift by the winds of the mind,

Each memory is a granule of moments passed but yet not easily left behind,

Many cling to the dust causing them to dwell on past pains or pleasures they find,

But life in a memory is only a shadow and lacks the power of the moment in its prime

Set the mind to purpose and soon fruits will be born
from the seeds of your labor,

Life is a fertile soil waiting to be nurtured and cultivated
by steadfast hands of sheer will,

Change is inevitable and control is an illusion yet any
who make the effort can still bear influence upon the
seeds they sow,

Reap the benefits of tenacious effort as your toil leads
to satisfying results of successful growth

The sweet scent of wildflowers permeates the surrounding air as beautiful blooms expand ever outward,

Above the colorful fields a blue sky reveals itself without limits as it bestows an awe inspiring view,

A chance encounter with such a blissful paradise offers a moment to let go of expectations and just be free,

To find such delight in nature's grasp is a welcome feeling that anyone can appreciate and happily embrace

Dreaming is an art form that if forgotten comes with great cost,

Some don't recognize the symbols in dreams that occur through the night as they turn and they toss,

It's time to remember the language of dreams that to so many seems lost,

Our dreams can teach us about ourselves so that deeper fears and insecurities we can accost

The mind can be opened or closed much like a window,

If closed, thoughts become stagnant with nowhere to go,

When opened it can provide fresh ideas to contemplate and to know,

It all depends on how much the individual wants to learn and to grow

Others can be cruel if unchecked when allowed, but you must rise above the fear of being judged by the crowd,

You are a magnificent sight, so stand strong and stand proud,

Let the strength of your spirit sound your authenticity aloud,

Hold your head high in the face of others as you remain unbowed

Open up your heart as your dreams come to light
shining for the world to see,

Dare to be inspired by the beauty found all around you
and within you,

It's easy to be sorrowful in the face of struggle and
hardship but being joyful creates far better results,

The world is yours for the taking if you grasp with all
your might and rise to the occasion as you best the
tribulations that you face on your journey in life

A dream begins its influence as it originates from the unconscious within one's psyche,

Expressions form as symbols try to reveal unexplored aspects of one's being,

The dream speaks a language of subtlety that one must decipher in order to know its full meaning,

A message to thyself waits to be decoded in the various tones of depth within the dreams mythic presentation,

Rewards of personal growth are experienced through the unraveling of the dream's teachings as a greater understanding of one's self develops

Darkness rises over the horizon as a storm churns in the ominous clouds above,

Drops of rain begin to pour from the weeping sky onto all beneath it and provide much needed water to the surrounding flora and fauna,

Lightning bolts surge and streak across the darkened sky as deafening thunderous roars echo forth,

The storm insights humility through the recognition of its magnitude and raw power it displays with intense ferocity

Meet the wind at its highest height among mountain peaks, as it whirls its whispers,

Meet the water at its rushing current where it will sweep you up in its arms and carry you swiftly,

Meet the Earth in its deepest caverns which surround you in its fortitude and fill you with awareness of its silent significance,

Meet the fire in its raging center where destruction and creation exist in a euphoric unity of ancient passion setting the world ablaze while simultaneously reshaping it anew,

Meet these elements as they manifest inward as aspects of your own nature and merge with the profound essence of your being

Fleeting gestures from external sources float by as the mind turns inward toward self-excavation,

Outer influences fade as inner workings of the self become clear and the depth of one's being reveals itself in seemingly unending proportions,

A universe of unfathomable power rests at the center of one's consciousness deep within,

To let go of what's outside ourselves and dive into the depth inside is a momentous occasion that offers a treasured taste of awakening that words can not fully express

Sometimes one must lose everything before they can truly gain anything,

It is all too common a practice to take for granted the profound lives we live,

One harsh bump in the road or one unwanted outcome can cause a great feeling of loss,

Yet when one can find hope while enduring suffering it is truly a wondrous act worthy of admiration,

To be human is to live out the beautiful scope of happiness and sadness and experience the full spectrum of being that lies between the two

You create the story that tells the tale of your life,

If you don't like the plot you have the power within to change the plot that you write,

You can overcome your problems and rise above your story's plight,

Open your eyes to your own potential and marvel at the sight

Every journey one takes in life begins with a single
step,

Many have walked paths of hardship and some feel
gratitude while others feel regret,

But even if yours is a difficult path you need not give
up yet,

The greater the trials the greater the rewards, just make
sure in stone, your will is set

The end is never truly the end as you shall see my friend,

The rabbits hole will only go deeper as it twists and turns and bends,

Along your beautiful journey in life just be honest and don't pretend,

If you ever need words of hope or encouragement, to you my words I lend